CW0064509

INCREDIBLE
MILITARY WEAPONS

by Tammy Gagne

Content Consultant
Mitchell A. Yockelson
Adjunct Faculty
US Naval Academy

Core Library

An Imprint of Abdo Publishing
www.abdopublishing.com

www.abdopublishing.com

Published by Abdo Publishing, a division of ABDO, PO Box 398166, Minneapolis, Minnesota 55439. Copyright © 2015 by Abdo Consulting Group, Inc. International copyrights reserved in all countries. No part of this book may be reproduced in any form without written permission from the publisher. Core Library™ is a trademark and logo of Abdo Publishing.

Printed in the United States of America, North Mankato, Minnesota
092014
012015

THIS BOOK CONTAINS
RECYCLED MATERIALS

Cover Photo: Spc. Ian Boudreau, 27th Infantry Brigade Combat Team Public Affairs/US Department of Defense
Interior Photos: Spc. Ian Boudreau, 27th Infantry Brigade Combat Team Public Affairs/US Department of Defense, 1; Library of Congress, 4, 6, 20; National Archives/NARA via CNP/Newscom, 9; War/UPPA/Photoshot/Newscom, 10; Spc. William J. Taylor/US Department of Defense, 12; R.A. Lord/Library of Congress, 14; Gary Blakeley/Shutterstock Images, 16 (upper left); Shutterstock Images, 16 (upper right), 16 (lower left), 26; Vladimir Gjorgiev/Shutterstock Images, 16 (lower right); Mass Communication Specialist 3rd Class Shawnte Bryan/US Department of Defense, 17; Andrey Shirokov/Newscom, 19; Senior Airman Julianne Showalter/US Department of Defense, 22, 45; Staff Sgt. Brian Ferguson/US Department of Defense, 25; US Army/US Department of Defense, 28; AP Images, 31, 42, 43; Photographer's Mate 1st Class David A. Levy/US Department of Defense, 33; Mass Communication Specialist 1st Class Jason C. Swink/US Department of Defense, 36; Lt. Shannon Collins/US Air Force/US Department of Defense, 39

Editor: Patrick Donnelly
Series Designer: Becky Daum

Library of Congress Control Number: 2014944243

Cataloging-in-Publication Data
Gagne, Tammy.
 Incredible military weapons / Tammy Gagne.
   p. cm. -- (Ready for military action)
ISBN 978-1-62403-652-1 (lib. bdg.)
Includes bibliographical references and index.
1. United States. --Army--Artillery--Juvenile literature. 2. Artillery--Juvenile literature. 3. Military weapons--United States--Juvenile literature.   I. Title.
623.4--dc23

2014944243

CONTENTS

CHAPTER ONE

MAKING HISTORY

By the summer of 1945, World War II had been raging for nearly six years. But the Allied forces, including the United States, the United Kingdom, and the Soviet Union, had begun to take control. Germany had surrendered on the European front. Japan's leaders knew they couldn't win in the Pacific. But still, they refused to give up.

A mushroom cloud rose above Nagasaki, Japan, after a US bomber dropped an atomic bomb on the city.

US President
Harry S. Truman

Truman's Options

US President Harry S. Truman had a tough decision before him. The Soviet Union had joined the Allies fighting in Europe in 1941. But the Soviets had not yet declared war on Japan. Truman knew that their help could make all the difference. But for the moment Soviet leaders remained undecided.

Truman also knew that he could invade Japan. That might help end the war. But at what cost? More than 55,000 Americans had already died fighting the Japanese. An invasion would mean even more casualties. And it would extend the war. But Japanese Emperor Hirohito was refusing to surrender.

Ending the War

Truman's top concern was to end the war as soon as possible. Doing so would save the lives of many American soldiers. Truman also had access to the most powerful weapon the world had ever seen. The atomic bomb had only recently become ready for use. This nuclear weapon was thousands of

A Warning?

Some historians think that the United States had two goals in dropping the atomic bombs on Japan. The first was to end the war as quickly as possible. But the United States also might have wanted to show the Soviet Union the power of its military. Relations between the two countries were declining around this time. When the United States bombed Japan, it showed the Soviets that it had a weapon of mass destruction and that its leaders would use the weapon if necessary.

times more powerful than any other bomb that had come before. No other country had ever used such a devastating weapon. But that would change on August 6, 1945.

The five-ton (4.5-metric ton) atomic bomb was loaded onto the *Enola Gay*, a US B-29 bomber plane. The *Enola Gay* crew dropped the bomb on the Japanese city of Hiroshima. The weapon instantly destroyed four square miles (10 sq km) of the city. It killed approximately 70,000 people. Three days later the US military dropped a second atomic bomb. It wiped out much of the city of Nagasaki. This attack killed approximately 40,000

The Manhattan Project

It took more than 100,000 scientists to develop the atomic bomb. The top-secret effort was called the Manhattan Project. Begun in 1942, the project included research done in 37 different locations around the United States. The scientists were among the best in the world. By 1945 they had completed their mission. The atomic bomb was ready for use.

Workers load "Fat Man," the atomic bomb dropped on Nagasaki, Japan, onto a trailer.

more Japanese people. In the next few months, more than 100,000 Japanese died from injuries and radiation poisoning. On September 2, 1945, the Japanese finally surrendered.

Years later, people still argue about the atomic bomb. Did Truman make the right decision? Was ending the war worth killing so many people? How many more lives would have been lost if the United States had not bombed Japan? No one can answer any of these questions with absolute certainty. But

Colonel Paul Tibbets stands next to his plane, the *Enola Gay*.

without these incredible weapons, World War II might have gone on for much longer.

Still, most people hope to avoid using nuclear bombs again in the future. Advancements in technology have helped create a variety of powerful new weapons. Some are so small they can fit in a soldier's hands. Others are so large they must be carried by vehicles. Each one plays a special role in modern warfare.

People still hold strong opinions about the bombings of Hiroshima and Nagasaki. The Scottish newspaper the *Herald* printed a letter to the editor written by Glasgow, Scotland, citizen George Quail in 2014 about the debate:

> It seems to me that whether or not nuclear weapons are morally wrong, they were undeniably effective at the goal Mr. Truman sought for them, since the very day after the bombings Prime Minister Suzuki met with the Emperor and essentially agreed to accept the terms of surrender. It is true that the matter of the Emperor's position post-surrender was a concession not made until a few days later, but otherwise complete acceptance of the terms hardly suggest people who were unmoved by the destruction wreaked upon them. The Russians may have helped seal the deal, but Hiroshima and Nagasaki were hardly [a] worthless sideshow.

> Source: George Quail. "Do not underestimate the role of the A-bomb in ending the war." The Herald. The Herald (Glasgow, Scotland), June 5, 2014. Web. Accessed September 25, 2014.

Back It Up

The author of this passage is making a point about the use of the atomic bomb in 1945. Write a paragraph describing the point the author is making. Be sure to include two or three pieces of evidence the author uses to make the point.

CHAPTER TWO

SMALL YET POWERFUL

Military weapons don't have to be big to be powerful. One of the most important weapons soldiers have is their sidearm. This is the weapon they carry at all times. Several hundred years ago, a sidearm might have been a dagger or a sword. Today's sidearms are guns, usually pistols. Guns allow soldiers to defend themselves from a greater distance than blades.

The pistol is the most common sidearm in the modern US military.

A Civil War–era soldier holds a musket equipped with a bayonet.

Early Small Arms

In the American Civil War (1861–1865) officers carried sidearms and sabers. But soldiers carried long guns called muskets. Most were equipped with a special blade on the muzzle called a bayonet. It gave soldiers two means of defense. Muskets could be used to shoot at distant enemies. Bayonets were useful in hand-to-hand fighting. Today the bayonet may be considered outdated. But every US Marine is still trained to use this deadly weapon.

By the early 1900s every US soldier was issued an M1911 pistol. This weapon offered several advantages. It was lightweight, easy to handle, and accurate. However, it held fewer than a dozen bullets, or rounds. The US military replaced the M1911 with the M9 Beretta in 1985. The change doubled the amount of ammunition a soldier's sidearm could hold. But many in the military resisted the change, as the M1911 was the more powerful weapon.

Sniper Rifles

Among the most important small arms are sniper rifles. These guns, such as the Barrett 82A1, are known for being extremely accurate from long distances. Special forces such as US Navy SEALs use sniper rifles to take down the most dangerous enemies. Some members of the army and marines also use them. The 82A1 has been used for more than 30 years and is still popular. Of course, any gun is only as accurate as the person firing it. But for a trained sniper, any target within a half-mile (0.8 km) is in range.

M1911 (1911–1985)	**Beretta M9** (1985–present)

Ammunition: .45 caliber	Ammunition: 9 mm

Standard-Issue Sidearms

Designed specifically for the US military, the M1911 had an impressively long service period. As the graphic above shows, the Beretta M9 holds more ammunition, while the M1911 fires a more powerful round. If you were a soldier, which sidearm would you prefer to carry? Why?

Carbine Rifles

In World War II a soldier's main weapon was the rifle. American soldiers carried M1 carbines at this time. Carbines have shorter barrels than other rifles. Although long guns were more powerful, they could be difficult to use in confined spaces. Moving around

Marines firing M4 carbine assault rifles

corners with them was particularly hard. Bigger weapons also are easier for the enemy to spot. That could give away a hiding soldier's position. The carbine rifle's shorter length solved both problems.

Today many US soldiers carry M4 carbine rifles. This weapon is capable of hitting targets up close or from 500 yards (460 m) away. The M4 carbine allows soldiers to fight the enemy whether near or far.

Problem Solved!

Since 2001 many US troops have served in the Middle East, particularly in Afghanistan and Iraq. They soon noticed a problem with their weapons. In the deserts of the Middle East, sand is everywhere. The grit was getting into the soldiers' M4 rifles. And it was jamming them. Something had to be done. Weapons that jammed were undependable. The HK416 provided a smart solution. This rifle is easier to maintain than the M4. For this reason many troops now carry the HK416 instead.

Big Advances in Small Weapons

An M320 grenade launcher turns the M4 carbine into an even more destructive weapon. A grenade launcher can be attached to another weapon, such as a rifle. It can hurl a grenade farther than a person can throw one. Each round the rifle fires can hit a single target. But mounting the M320 onto the M4 creates an even more powerful weapon. With the M320 a soldier can also fire a grenade more than 400 yards (370 m). And that grenade can blast an area of up to 850 square feet

The CornerShot allows shooters to see and fire at a target around corners.

(80 sq m). The M320 and other grenade launchers can also be used without the M4.

Other useful small arms include the CornerShot and the XM25 rifle. The CornerShot weapons system has a small video camera and screen. A hinge allows the soldier to turn the gun. This unique weapon makes it possible to fire around corners. The XM25 rifle shoots through walls. Its ammunition can be programmed to explode after it makes it to the other side of the wall.

CHAPTER THREE

LOCKED AND LOADED— AND LARGE

The US military has some impressive small weapons in its arsenal. But sometimes a larger weapon is necessary. Many wars have been won with the help of large guns, rockets, and even some military vehicles that double as weapons.

True Transformers

It is easy to think of planes and helicopters merely as transportation. After all, these vehicles carry soldiers

Soldiers pose next to an American Civil War cannon.

The AC-130U Spooky fires defensive flares as a countermeasure against heat-seeking missiles.

from one location to another. But sometimes an aircraft can serve as a large weapon itself.

At first glance the AC-130U Spooky looks like a regular cargo plane. But it is actually a gunship. The Spooky is equipped with three large weapons. Each AC-130U carries a machine gun that weighs 270 pounds (120 kg) and has five barrels. It also carries a 105mm cannon and a 40mm cannon.

It isn't just its firepower that makes the Spooky an incredible weapon. The AC130 was specially designed for lengthy nighttime attacks. The plane's sensors can locate targets on the ground and tell friendly forces apart from enemy troops. The Spooky's sensors even allow it to carry out missions in poor weather.

The AH-64D Apache Longbow is a helicopter. But it isn't just any helicopter. Like the Spooky, this aircraft was designed for nighttime attacks in a variety of weather. In addition to a 30mm cannon, the Longbow also has 70mm rockets. The helicopter's radar can assess up to 128 targets in less than a minute.

The Javelin Missile

The FGM-148 Javelin is a portable missile launcher used by US troops to destroy tanks. The Javelin finds an enemy tank by detecting its heat. After being fired, the missile flies high into the air above its target. It then dives straight down and hits the top of the tank, where its armor is relatively weak.

Bringing in the Big Guns

Soldiers traveling by land can't carry weapons the size of cannons. But they can use large trucks to tow them. Some weapons, such as some howitzers, can move by themselves. These short guns look like cannons and fire shells high into the air.

One of the most incredible things about the howitzer is how long it has been around. This type of field artillery piece has been in use since the 1600s, when it was invented by the Dutch. What makes modern howitzers special is their range. The Howitzer

MQ-9 Reaper Drone

The MQ-9 Reaper drone is a remote-control airplane. This unmanned aircraft allows the US military to fly into areas where pilots would not be safe. The MQ-9's main purpose is gathering information. But it can also strike a target with AGM-114 Hellfire missiles if needed. A specially trained pilot focuses on flying the plane. A second aircrew member operates the sensors and weapon systems. Both tasks can be performed from more than 1,000 miles (1,600 km) away.

The MQ-9 Reaper drone can be piloted by troops more than 1,000 miles (1,600 km) away.

M777 can hit a target with 155-mm shells from approximately 20 miles (32 km) away.

And the technology is still moving forward. When the M777 uses a satellite-guided artillery shell, its range increases. These shells have been proven to strike within approximately 30 feet (10 m) of a target when fired from 25 miles (40 km) away.

Another large yet mobile weapon is the Multiple Launch Rocket System (MLRS). This weapon is another example of a vehicle that acts as a weapon. At first glance the MLRS looks like a tank. That is no accident.

AGM-114
Hellfire Missile

Hydra 70
Rockets

30mm M230
Chain Gun
Rounds

AH-64 Apache Helicopters

The US military uses three different AH-64 Apache
helicopters. The AH-64 was the original of the three. The
AH-64D Longbow was added in 1997. Above, an AH-64 is
shown with three different types of weapons that it carries.

This is based on the M270 Bradley Fighting Vehicle. It
fires surface-to-surface rockets and missiles at targets
as far away as 30 miles (48 km).

M1 Abrams tanks are another example of a vehicle that doubles as a weapon. They have been in use for more than 30 years. But these large weapons might be on their way out of service.

> In the last decade . . . as hundreds [of Abrams] were deployed to Iraq and later Afghanistan, a key shortcoming became apparent: Their flat bottoms made the Abrams surprisingly vulnerable to improvised explosive devices (IEDs). As a result, the Abrams in Iraq ended up being used as "pillboxes"— high-priced armored bunkers used to protect ground.

> "The M1 is an extraordinary vehicle, the best tank on the planet," Paul D. Eaton, a retired Army major general now with the nonprofit National Security Network, said in an interview. Since the primary purpose of tanks is to kill other tanks, however, their utility in modern counterinsurgency warfare is limited, he added.

> Source: "The M1 Abrams: The Army tank that could not be stopped." NBC News Investigations. NBCNews.com, July 28, 2012. Web. Accessed August 7, 2014.

What's the Big Idea?

Take a close look at this passage. What is the main point? Pick out two details that support your opinion. What does the story suggest about the future of Abrams tanks?

CHAPTER FOUR

EXPLOSIVES

Hundreds of years ago the most remarkable weapon any military had was the cannon. This large piece of artillery was certainly effective. But it was also heavy. A popular French cannon from the mid-1700s was called the four-pounder. It was named for the weight of the solid iron balls it fired. But the cannon itself weighed a whopping

Patriot missiles are designed to intercept enemy aircraft and missiles before they reach their intended targets.

784 pounds (356 kg). Even on wheels, this weapon was basically stationary.

Explosive weapons have become more powerful than ever in the 2000s. The US military can send missiles and other self-propelled explosives many miles. Troops can launch these devices from either land or sea. And some are surprisingly lightweight and mobile.

Daisy Cutters

Daisy Cutter bombs have been around since the Vietnam War (1959–1975). The United States began using them again in Afghanistan in 2001. Nicknamed for the flowerlike pattern they leave behind, Daisy Cutters are among the biggest nonnuclear bombs the US military uses. Each one weighs approximately 15,000 pounds (6,800 kg) and is roughly the size of an automobile.

Patriot Missiles

One of the most advanced explosive weapons today is the Patriot missile system. Its speed and range make it ideal for defending against air attacks. A Patriot missile can travel up to 44 miles (70 km) at supersonic speed. It can hit and

The 15,000-pound (6,800-kg) Daisy Cutter is one of the largest nonnuclear bombs in the US military arsenal.

destroy advanced aircraft before they come within a dangerous range. It can even stop other guided missiles, such as ballistic missiles and cruise missiles, in midair.

As powerful as the Patriot already is, engineers continue to work on it. Early versions could only throw an incoming missile off course. But today the Patriot can destroy its targets so they cannot do damage anywhere. The Patriot's range is continually being improved. The US military expects it to remain in service until at least 2048.

Fuel-Air Explosives

Whereas Patriot missiles are used for air defense, fuel-air explosives help the military destroy threats on the ground. When dropped from an aircraft, these weapons release clouds of fuel. At the center of each device is a detonator that ignites the fuel. The result is a devastating explosion that can flatten everything in its area.

Fuel-air explosives can wipe out armored vehicles, bunkers, and minefields. They can even destroy aircraft parked on the ground. By removing these threats, these incredible weapons help protect ground troops in the area from the enemy.

A Real Blast

Fuel-air explosives work well for destroying visible targets. But to reach hidden targets, the military often relies on C4, a type of plastic explosive. Troops

Troops can mold C4 explosive into different shapes to suit their demolition needs.

often use C4 to blast through heavy walls. But it can be used to blow up almost anything. This substance, which looks like a block of modeling clay, is highly portable. Soldiers can carry C4 in their pockets if necessary. Only 1.25 pounds (0.5 kg) of the explosive is enough to blow up a truck.

The effect of C4 is a lot like that of dynamite. But C4 offers several advantages. Soldiers can mold this soft material into different shapes. It can be packed into cracks or holes. Each piece of C4 is wrapped in paper with a sticky side. This feature allows soldiers to place the explosive on almost any surface.

One of the most incredible things about C4 is that it is surprisingly safe to handle. It won't explode from being dropped, set on fire, or even shot with a regular bullet. It will only blow up when triggered by a special detonation device. Unfortunately, the very things that make C4 such a great weapon for the US military also make it appealing to the enemy. Terrorists frequently use this explosive in their attacks.

EXPLORE ONLINE

Go to the website below and find the article about advances in military explosives. How does it compare to what you read in Chapter Four? Write a paragraph about the differences between TNT, IMX-101 and C4. Which do you think is safest? Why?

Finding Safer Explosives
www.mycorelibrary.com/weapons

CHAPTER FIVE

SMART WEAPONS

As technology advances, weapons are getting smarter. The bullets and cannon balls of the past had to be aimed and fired by a person. But weapons like today's cruise missiles guide themselves to their targets. That means these modern missiles have a much better chance of reaching their targets.

A Tomahawk cruise missile is loaded onto a submarine for transport.

Heat-Seeking Technology

Heat-seeking missiles like the AIM-9 Sidewinder have been around since the 1950s. How do they work? These special weapons are equipped with computer devices that search for radiation. Whether on land or in the air, engines in planes, helicopters, and other vehicles become hot as they operate. Heat-seeking missiles use that heat to identify a vehicle's location. Once the heat is found, the computers use it to guide the missile to the machine emitting it.

The first so-called smart bombs were used in the Vietnam War. An F-4 fighter plane equipped with a laser would identify a target area. Bomber aircraft would then drop bombs into the marked area. Success depended on how well the pilots did at pointing out the right location. It then rested on the bomber pilots to release their weapons at the perfect moment.

At that point it was the best system the US Air Force had ever had. But it still left plenty of room for error. Civilians may have been killed because bombs were dropped just a bit too early or late.

The AIM-9 Sidewinder uses heat-seeking technology and special fins to steer it toward its target.

Cruise Missiles

Today cruise missiles, or Tomahawks, can do several things the Vietnam War pilots could not. Even small planes need a great deal of fuel to stay in the air. F-4 pilots sometimes had to refuel to reach their targets and get back to their bases. Tomahawks, on the other hand, can stay in the air for hours.

The troops directing cruise missiles can be more than 1,000 miles (1,600 km) away from the danger zone. But they can still see everything that happens.

Antisubmarine Aircraft

Technology has helped the military find the enemy in some remote locations. But how does one spot a military vehicle underwater? Antisubmarine aircraft were designed for this purpose. The latest in this line of antisubmarine warfare is the P-8A Poseidon. It is capable of locating enemy subs lurking below the ocean's surface. The Poseidon is equipped with Mk 54 lightweight torpedoes. These powerful missiles can destroy targets in both deep and shallow water.

The missile can send pictures of its target instantly to a computer. If needed, the people firing the missile can change its course. The weapon is guided to its target by the Global Positioning System.

Joint Direct Attack Munitions

Military engineers have found a way to turn regular bombs into smart ones. The Joint Direct Attack Munition is better known as JDAM. This guidance kit attaches to a free-fall bomb's tail section. The kit provides the bomb with GPS technology. Special fins help steer the bomb toward its target.

The JDAM kit helps the military stretch its budget. Each Tomahawk missile costs more than $1 million. But a JDAM kit costs only approximately $20,000. Even after adding the price of the bomb itself, this incredible technology is a huge bargain for the US military.

Military weapons have come a long way over the last century. And with improved technology, they are sure to progress even further as time moves forward.

FURTHER EVIDENCE

Chapter Five includes a lot of information about some of the US military's newest weapons. What is the main point of this chapter? What key evidence supports this point? Go to the website below and find the article about the US Army's gear and weapons. Does the information support the main point in this chapter? Write a few sentences using new information from the website as evidence to support the main point in this chapter.

Army Gear and Weapons
www.mycorelibrary.com/weapons

Fidel Castro

The Bay of Pigs, 1961

In 1961 a group of Cuban rebels, called Brigade 2506, set out to remove dictator Fidel Castro from power. The US Central Intelligence Agency funded the mission. The group hoped to rally the citizens of Cuba to overthrow the government. The invading soldiers carried M1 carbines. They also brought mortars of various sizes with them. But Castro's military defeated the rebels with little effort. The Cuban military quickly sank the group's ships. More than 100 of the soldiers were killed. Another 1,100 were captured.

Osama bin Laden

Osama bin Laden, 2011

One of the most famous military missions in American history was the capture of terrorist Osama bin Laden. A Special Forces group known as US Navy SEAL Team Six found the man responsible for the terrorist attacks in the United States on September 11, 2001. Dozens of SEALs boarded four Blackhawk helicopters and ambushed the terrorist at his compound in Abbottabad, Pakistan. No one knows which team member killed bin Laden. But the job was done with a HK416 rifle.

STOP AND THINK

Take a Stand

In Chapter One you learned about the atomic bombs dropped on Hiroshima and Nagasaki. Imagine that you were a general in the US military near the end of World War II. Write a letter to President Truman explaining what you think he should do to bring an end to the war.

Surprise Me

Technology has turned weaponry into a constantly changing industry. Some of the weapons that exist today could not even be imagined 100 years ago. Which weapon described in this book do you think is the most incredible? Why? What do you think American Civil War soldiers would have thought about this modern weapon?

Say What?

The US military uses words that are new to many civilians. Make a list of five new words you learned from reading this book and write down their definitions. If your word isn't in the glossary, use a dictionary to find the meaning instead.

You Are There

Imagine that you are a pilot in control of an MQ-9 Reaper. Write a story about your mission. What is your goal? What do you see? Even though you are far away from the plane itself, are you nervous?

GLOSSARY

arsenal
a place for the manufacture or storage of arms

artillery
large guns that are used to shoot over a great distance

ballistic
dealing with the motion of falling objects

caliber
the inside diameter of a gun barrel

carbine
a light short-barreled rifle

casualties
people lost (as by death or capture) during warfare

detonator
a device or small quantity of explosive used for detonating another explosive

grenade
a small bomb designed to be thrown by hand or launched (as by a rifle)

howitzer
a short cannon capable of firing a shell in a high arc

rounds
ammunition

supersonic
faster than the speed of sound

LEARN MORE

Books

McNab, Chris. *A History of the World in 100 Weapons*. Oxford, England: Osprey Publishing, 2014.

Military History: The Definitive Visual Guide to the Objects of Warfare. Washington, DC: DK Publishing, 2012.

Websites

To learn more about the US military and its resources, visit **booklinks.abdopublishing.com**. These links are routinely monitored and updated to provide the most current information available.

Visit **www.mycorelibrary.com** for free additional tools for teachers and students.

INDEX

ABOUT THE AUTHOR

Tammy Gagne has written more than 100 books for both adults and children. She resides in northern New England with her husband and son. One of her favorite pastimes is visiting schools to talk to children about the writing process.